Readi

Reading is a means of thinking with another's person mind.It forces you to stretch your own.

Charles Scribner Jr

This Log belongs to:

. . . .

 READING LOG BOOK

NO.	BOOK TITLE	AUTHOR	RATING
1.			☆☆☆☆☆
2.			☆☆☆☆☆
3.			☆☆☆☆☆
4.			☆☆☆☆☆
5.			☆☆☆☆☆
6.			☆☆☆☆☆
7.			☆☆☆☆☆
8.			☆☆☆☆☆
9.			☆☆☆☆☆
10.			☆☆☆☆☆
11.			☆☆☆☆☆
12.			☆☆☆☆☆
13.			☆☆☆☆☆
14.			☆☆☆☆☆
15.			☆☆☆☆☆
16.			☆☆☆☆☆
17.			☆☆☆☆☆
18.			☆☆☆☆☆
19.			☆☆☆☆☆
20.			☆☆☆☆☆

 READING LOG BOOK

NO.	BOOK TITLE	AUTHOR	RATING
21.			☆☆☆☆☆
22.			☆☆☆☆☆
23.			☆☆☆☆☆
24.			☆☆☆☆☆
25.			☆☆☆☆☆
26.			☆☆☆☆☆
27.			☆☆☆☆☆
28.			☆☆☆☆☆
29.			☆☆☆☆☆
30.			☆☆☆☆☆
31.			☆☆☆☆☆
32.			☆☆☆☆☆
33.			☆☆☆☆☆
34.			☆☆☆☆☆
35.			☆☆☆☆☆
36.			☆☆☆☆☆
37.			☆☆☆☆☆
38.			☆☆☆☆☆
39.			☆☆☆☆☆
40.			☆☆☆☆☆

READING LOG BOOK

NO.	BOOK TITLE	AUTHOR	RATING
41.			☆☆☆☆☆
42.			☆☆☆☆☆
43.			☆☆☆☆☆
44.			☆☆☆☆☆
45.			☆☆☆☆☆
46.			☆☆☆☆☆
47.			☆☆☆☆☆
48.			☆☆☆☆☆
49.			☆☆☆☆☆
50.			☆☆☆☆☆
51.			☆☆☆☆☆
52.			☆☆☆☆☆
53.			☆☆☆☆☆
54.			☆☆☆☆☆
55.			☆☆☆☆☆
56.			☆☆☆☆☆
57.			☆☆☆☆☆
58.			☆☆☆☆☆
59.			☆☆☆☆☆
60.			☆☆☆☆☆

 READING LOG BOOK

NO.	BOOK TITLE	AUTHOR	RATING
61.			☆☆☆☆☆
62.			☆☆☆☆☆
63.			☆☆☆☆☆
64.			☆☆☆☆☆
65.			☆☆☆☆☆
66.			☆☆☆☆☆
67.			☆☆☆☆☆
68.			☆☆☆☆☆
69.			☆☆☆☆☆
70.			☆☆☆☆☆
71.			☆☆☆☆☆
72.			☆☆☆☆☆
73.			☆☆☆☆☆
74.			☆☆☆☆☆
75.			☆☆☆☆☆
76.			☆☆☆☆☆
77.			☆☆☆☆☆
78.			☆☆☆☆☆
79.			☆☆☆☆☆
80.			☆☆☆☆☆

 **READING LOG BOOK**

NO.	BOOK TITLE	AUTHOR	RATING
81.			☆☆☆☆☆
82.			☆☆☆☆☆
83.			☆☆☆☆☆
84.			☆☆☆☆☆
85.			☆☆☆☆☆
86.			☆☆☆☆☆
87.			☆☆☆☆☆
88.			☆☆☆☆☆
89.			☆☆☆☆☆
90.			☆☆☆☆☆
91.			☆☆☆☆☆
92.			☆☆☆☆☆
93.			☆☆☆☆☆
94.			☆☆☆☆☆
95.			☆☆☆☆☆
96.			☆☆☆☆☆
97.			☆☆☆☆☆
98.			☆☆☆☆☆
99.			☆☆☆☆☆
100.			☆☆☆☆☆

TITLE: _____ PUB DATE: _____

AUTHOR: _____ PAGE COUNT: _____

DATE STARTED: _____ DATE FINISHED: _____

SOURCE: _____ Bought ☐ Loaned ☐

Fiction ☐   Non-fiction ☐

GENRE:		☆☆☆☆☆
SUBJECT:		☆☆☆☆☆
CHARACTERS:		☆☆☆☆☆
PLOT:		☆☆☆☆☆☆
READABILITY SCORE:		☆☆☆☆☆

Inspiration tree

Why I read it?

☆ MY REVIEW:

It inspired me to:

Who will I
recommend it
to?

_____
_____
_____
_____
_____
_____
_____
_____
_____
_____

FAVORITE QUOTES FROM THIS BOOK:

hardcover   paperback   ebook   audiobook

OVERALL RATING: ☆☆☆☆☆

TITLE: _____ PUB DATE: _____

AUTHOR: _____ PAGE COUNT: _____

DATE STARTED: _____ DATE FINISHED: _____

SOURCE: _____ Bought ☐ Loaned ☐

Fiction ☐ Non-fiction ☐

GENRE:		☆☆☆☆☆
SUBJECT:		☆☆☆☆☆
CHARACTERS:		☆☆☆☆☆
PLOT:		☆☆☆☆☆
READABILITY SCORE:		☆☆☆☆☆

Inspiration tree

Why I read it?

☆ MY REVIEW:

It inspired me to:

_____
_____
_____
_____

Who will I recommend it to?

_____
_____
_____
_____
_____

FAVORITE QUOTES FROM THIS BOOK:

hardcover   paperback   ebook   audiobook

OVERALL RATING: ☆☆☆☆☆

TITLE: _____ PUB DATE: _____

AUTHOR: _____ PAGE COUNT: _____

DATE STARTED: _____ DATE FINISHED: _____

SOURCE: _____ Bought ☐ Loaned ☐

Fiction ☐   Non-fiction ☐

GENRE:		☆☆☆☆☆
SUBJECT:		☆☆☆☆☆
CHARACTERS:		☆☆☆☆☆
PLOT:		☆☆☆☆☆
READABILITY SCORE:		☆☆☆☆☆

Inspiration tree

Why I read it?

☆ MY REVIEW:

It inspired me to:

_____

_____

_____

Who will I
recommend it
to?

_____

_____

_____

_____

_____

FAVORITE QUOTES FROM THIS BOOK:

hardcover   paperback   ebook   audiobook

OVERALL RATING: ☆☆☆☆☆

TITLE: ———————————————— PUB DATE: ————————

AUTHOR: ——————————————— PAGE COUNT: ——————

DATE STARTED: ————————— DATE FINISHED: ————

SOURCE: ——————————————— Bought ☐ Loaned ☐

Fiction ☐ Non-fiction ☐

GENRE:		☆☆☆☆☆
SUBJECT:		☆☆☆☆☆
CHARACTERS:		☆☆☆☆☆
PLOT:		☆☆☆☆☆
READABILITY SCORE:		☆☆☆☆☆

Inspiration tree

Why I read it?

☆ MY REVIEW:

It inspired me to:

Who will I
recommend it
to?

FAVORITE QUOTES FROM THIS BOOK:

hardcover   paperback   ebook   audiobook

OVERALL RATING: ☆☆☆☆☆

TITLE: ──────────────── PUB DATE: ────────

AUTHOR: ─────────────── PAGE COUNT: ──────

DATE STARTED: ────────── DATE FINISHED: ──────

SOURCE: ───────────────

Bought ☐   Loaned ☐

Fiction ☐   Non-fiction ☐

GENRE:		☆☆☆☆☆
SUBJECT:		☆☆☆☆☆
CHARACTERS:		☆☆☆☆☆
PLOT:		☆☆☆☆☆
READABILITY SCORE:		☆☆☆☆☆

Inspiration tree

Why I read it?

☆ MY REVIEW:

It inspired me to:

Who will I recommend it to?

_____

_____

_____

_____

_____

_____

_____

_____

_____

_____

FAVORITE QUOTES FROM THIS BOOK:

hardcover   paperback   ebook   audiobook

OVERALL RATING: ☆☆☆☆☆

TITLE: ——————————— PUB DATE: ———————

AUTHOR: ————————— PAGE COUNT: ————————

DATE STARTED: ——————— DATE FINISHED: ——————

SOURCE: ———————————

Bought ☐ Loaned ☐

Fiction ☐   Non-fiction ☐

GENRE:		☆☆☆☆☆
SUBJECT:		☆☆☆☆☆
CHARACTERS:		☆☆☆☆☆
PLOT:		☆☆☆☆☆
READABILITY SCORE:		☆☆☆☆☆

Inspiration tree

Why I read it?

☆ MY REVIEW:

It inspired me to:

Who will I
recommend it
to?

FAVORITE QUOTES FROM THIS BOOK:

hardcover   paperback   ebook   audiobook

OVERALL RATING: ☆☆☆☆☆

TITLE: _____   PUB DATE: _____

AUTHOR: _____   PAGE COUNT: _____

DATE STARTED: _____   DATE FINISHED: _____

SOURCE: _____   Bought ☐   Loaned ☐

Fiction ☐   Non-fiction ☐

GENRE:		☆☆☆☆☆
SUBJECT:		☆☆☆☆☆
CHARACTERS:		☆☆☆☆☆
PLOT:		☆☆☆☆☆
READABILITY SCORE:		☆☆☆☆☆

Inspiration tree

☆ MY REVIEW:

Why I read it?

It inspired me to:

Who will I
recommend it
to?

_____
_____
_____
_____
_____
_____
_____
_____
_____
_____

FAVORITE QUOTES FROM THIS BOOK:

hardcover   paperback   ebook   audiobook

OVERALL RATING: ☆☆☆☆☆

TITLE: _____ PUB DATE: _____

AUTHOR: _____ PAGE COUNT: _____

DATE STARTED: _____ DATE FINISHED: _____

SOURCE: _____ Bought ☐ Loaned ☐

Fiction ☐   Non-fiction ☐

GENRE:		☆☆☆☆☆
SUBJECT:		☆☆☆☆☆
CHARACTERS:		☆☆☆☆☆
PLOT:		☆☆☆☆☆
READABILITY SCORE:		☆☆☆☆☆

Inspiration tree

Why I read it?

☆ MY REVIEW:

It inspired me to:

_____
_____
_____
_____

Who will I
recommend it
to?

_____
_____
_____
_____
_____
_____

FAVORITE QUOTES FROM THIS BOOK:

hardcover   paperback   ebook   audiobook

OVERALL RATING: ☆☆☆☆☆

TITLE: _____   PUB DATE: _____

AUTHOR: _____   PAGE COUNT: _____

DATE STARTED: _____   DATE FINISHED: _____

SOURCE: _____   Bought ☐   Loaned ☐

Fiction ☐   Non-fiction ☐

GENRE:		☆☆☆☆☆
SUBJECT:		☆☆☆☆☆
CHARACTERS:		☆☆☆☆☆
PLOT:		☆☆☆☆☆
READABILITY SCORE:		☆☆☆☆☆

Inspiration tree

☆ MY REVIEW:

Why I read it?

_____

_____

_____

It inspired me to:

_____

_____

_____

Who will I recommend it to?

_____

_____

_____

_____

_____

FAVORITE QUOTES FROM THIS BOOK:

hardcover   paperback   ebook   audiobook

OVERALL RATING: ☆☆☆☆☆

TITLE: _____   PUB DATE: _____

AUTHOR: _____   PAGE COUNT: _____

DATE STARTED: _____   DATE FINISHED: _____

SOURCE: _____   Bought ☐   Loaned ☐

Fiction ☐   Non-fiction ☐

GENRE:		☆☆☆☆☆
SUBJECT:		☆☆☆☆☆
CHARACTERS:		☆☆☆☆☆
PLOT:		☆☆☆☆☆
READABILITY SCORE:		☆☆☆☆☆

Inspiration tree

Why I read it?

☆ MY REVIEW:

It inspired me to:

Who will I recommend it to?

_____
_____
_____
_____
_____
_____
_____
_____
_____
_____

FAVORITE QUOTES FROM THIS BOOK:

hardcover   paperback   ebook   audiobook

OVERALL RATING: ☆☆☆☆☆

TITLE: _____ PUB DATE: _____

AUTHOR: _____ PAGE COUNT: _____

DATE STARTED: _____ DATE FINISHED: _____

SOURCE: _____ Bought ☐ Loaned ☐

Fiction ☐   Non-fiction ☐

GENRE:		☆☆☆☆☆
SUBJECT:		☆☆☆☆☆
CHARACTERS:		☆☆☆☆☆
PLOT:		☆☆☆☆☆
READABILITY SCORE:		☆☆☆☆☆

Inspiration tree

☆ MY REVIEW:

Why I read it?

_____

_____

It inspired me to:

_____

_____

_____

Who will I
recommend it
to?

_____

_____

_____

_____

FAVORITE QUOTES FROM THIS BOOK:

hardcover   paperback   ebook   audiobook

OVERALL RATING: ☆☆☆☆☆

TITLE: _____   PUB DATE: _____

AUTHOR: _____   PAGE COUNT: _____

DATE STARTED: _____   DATE FINISHED: _____

SOURCE: _____

Bought ☐   Loaned ☐

Fiction ☐   Non-fiction ☐

GENRE:		☆☆☆☆☆
SUBJECT:		☆☆☆☆☆
CHARACTERS:		☆☆☆☆☆
PLOT:		☆☆☆☆☆
READABILITY SCORE:		☆☆☆☆☆

Inspiration tree

Why I read it?

☆ MY REVIEW:

It inspired me to:

Who will I recommend it to?

_____
_____
_____
_____
_____
_____
_____
_____
_____
_____
_____

FAVORITE QUOTES FROM THIS BOOK:

hardcover   paperback   ebook   audiobook

OVERALL RATING: ☆☆☆☆☆

TITLE: _____ PUB DATE: _____

AUTHOR: _____ PAGE COUNT: _____

DATE STARTED: _____ DATE FINISHED: _____

SOURCE: _____ Bought ☐ Loaned ☐

Fiction ☐   Non-fiction ☐

GENRE:		☆☆☆☆☆
SUBJECT:		☆☆☆☆☆
CHARACTERS:		☆☆☆☆☆
PLOT:		☆☆☆☆☆
READABILITY SCORE:		☆☆☆☆☆

Inspiration tree

Why I read it?

It inspired me to:

Who will I recommend it to?

☆ MY REVIEW:

_____
_____
_____
_____
_____
_____
_____
_____
_____
_____

FAVORITE QUOTES FROM THIS BOOK:

hardcover   paperback   ebook   audiobook

OVERALL RATING: ☆☆☆☆☆

TITLE: _____ PUB DATE: _____

AUTHOR: _____ PAGE COUNT: _____

DATE STARTED: _____ DATE FINISHED: _____

SOURCE: _____ Bought ☐ Loaned ☐

Fiction ☐   Non-fiction ☐

GENRE:		☆☆☆☆☆
SUBJECT:		☆☆☆☆☆
CHARACTERS:		☆☆☆☆☆
PLOT:		☆☆☆☆☆
READABILITY SCORE:		☆☆☆☆☆

Inspiration tree

Why I read it?

☆ MY REVIEW:

It inspired me to: _____
_____
_____
_____

Who will I recommend it to? _____
_____
_____
_____
_____
_____

FAVORITE QUOTES FROM THIS BOOK:

hardcover   paperback   ebook   audiobook

OVERALL RATING: ☆☆☆☆☆

TITLE: _____ PUB DATE: _____

AUTHOR: _____ PAGE COUNT: _____

DATE STARTED: _____ DATE FINISHED: _____

SOURCE: _____ Bought ☐   Loaned ☐

Fiction ☐   Non-fiction ☐

GENRE:		☆☆☆☆☆
SUBJECT:		☆☆☆☆☆
CHARACTERS:		☆☆☆☆☆
PLOT:		☆☆☆☆☆
READABILITY SCORE:		☆☆☆☆☆

Inspiration tree

Why I read it?

It inspired me to:

Who will I recommend it to?

⭐ MY REVIEW:

_____
_____
_____
_____
_____
_____
_____
_____
_____
_____

FAVORITE QUOTES FROM THIS BOOK:

hardcover   paperback   ebook   audiobook

OVERALL RATING: ☆☆☆☆☆

TITLE: ———————————— PUB DATE: ————

AUTHOR: ———————————— PAGE COUNT: ————

DATE STARTED: ———————— DATE FINISHED: ————

SOURCE: ———————————— Bought ☐ Loaned ☐

Fiction ☐   Non-fiction ☐

GENRE:		☆☆☆☆☆
SUBJECT:		☆☆☆☆☆
CHARACTERS:		☆☆☆☆☆
PLOT:		☆☆☆☆☆
READABILITY SCORE:		☆☆☆☆☆

Inspiration tree

Why I read it?

It inspired me to:

Who will I recommend it to?

☆ MY REVIEW:

_____

_____

_____

_____

_____

_____

_____

_____

_____

_____

FAVORITE QUOTES FROM THIS BOOK:

hardcover   paperback   ebook   audiobook

OVERALL RATING: ☆☆☆☆☆

TITLE: _____ PUB DATE: _____

AUTHOR: _____ PAGE COUNT: _____

DATE STARTED: _____ DATE FINISHED: _____

SOURCE: _____

Bought ☐   Loaned ☐

Fiction ☐   Non-fiction ☐

GENRE:		☆☆☆☆☆
SUBJECT:		☆☆☆☆☆
CHARACTERS:		☆☆☆☆☆
PLOT:		☆☆☆☆☆
READABILITY SCORE:		☆☆☆☆☆

Inspiration tree

Why I read it?

☆ MY REVIEW:

It inspired me to:

Who will I recommend it to?

_____
_____
_____
_____
_____
_____
_____
_____
_____
_____
_____

FAVORITE QUOTES FROM THIS BOOK:

hardcover   paperback   ebook   audiobook

OVERALL RATING: ☆☆☆☆☆

TITLE: _____ PUB DATE: _____

AUTHOR: _____ PAGE COUNT: _____

DATE STARTED: _____ DATE FINISHED: _____

SOURCE: _____ Bought ☐   Loaned ☐

Fiction ☐   Non-fiction ☐

GENRE:		☆☆☆☆☆
SUBJECT:		☆☆☆☆☆
CHARACTERS:		☆☆☆☆☆
PLOT:		☆☆☆☆☆
READABILITY SCORE:		☆☆☆☆☆

Inspiration tree

Why I read it?

☆ MY REVIEW:

It inspired me to:

Who will I recommend it to?

_____
_____
_____
_____
_____
_____
_____
_____
_____

FAVORITE QUOTES FROM THIS BOOK:

hardcover   paperback   ebook   audiobook

OVERALL RATING: ☆☆☆☆☆

TITLE: _____   PUB DATE: _____

AUTHOR: _____   PAGE COUNT: _____

DATE STARTED: _____   DATE FINISHED: _____

SOURCE: _____   Bought ☐   Loaned ☐

Fiction ☐   Non-fiction ☐

GENRE:		☆☆☆☆☆
SUBJECT:		☆☆☆☆☆
CHARACTERS:		☆☆☆☆☆
PLOT:		☆☆☆☆☆
READABILITY SCORE:		☆☆☆☆☆

Inspiration tree

Why I read it?

☆ MY REVIEW:

It inspired me to:

_____

_____

_____

_____

Who will I
recommend it
to?

_____

_____

_____

_____

FAVORITE QUOTES FROM THIS BOOK:

hardcover   paperback   ebook   audiobook

OVERALL RATING: ☆☆☆☆☆

TITLE: _____ PUB DATE: _____

AUTHOR: _____ PAGE COUNT: _____

DATE STARTED: _____ DATE FINISHED: _____

SOURCE: _____ Bought ☐ Loaned ☐

Fiction ☐   Non-fiction ☐

GENRE:		☆☆☆☆☆
SUBJECT:		☆☆☆☆☆
CHARACTERS:		☆☆☆☆☆
PLOT:		☆☆☆☆☆
READABILITY SCORE:		☆☆☆☆☆

Inspiration tree

Why I read it?

☆ MY REVIEW:

It inspired me to:

_____
_____
_____
_____
_____

Who will I
recommend it
to?

_____
_____
_____
_____
_____

FAVORITE QUOTES FROM THIS BOOK:

hardcover   paperback   ebook   audiobook

OVERALL RATING: ☆☆☆☆☆

TITLE: _____ PUB DATE: _____

AUTHOR: _____ PAGE COUNT: _____

DATE STARTED: _____ DATE FINISHED: _____

SOURCE: _____ Bought ☐   Loaned ☐

Fiction ☐   Non-fiction ☐

GENRE:		☆☆☆☆☆
SUBJECT:		☆☆☆☆☆
CHARACTERS:		☆☆☆☆☆
PLOT:		☆☆☆☆☆
READABILITY SCORE:		☆☆☆☆☆

Inspiration tree

Why I read it?

☆ MY REVIEW:

It inspired me to:

Who will I recommend it to?

FAVORITE QUOTES FROM THIS BOOK:

hardcover   paperback   ebook   audiobook

OVERALL RATING: ☆☆☆☆☆

TITLE: _____ PUB DATE: _____

AUTHOR: _____ PAGE COUNT: _____

DATE STARTED: _____ DATE FINISHED: _____

SOURCE: _____ Bought ☐ Loaned ☐

Fiction ☐ Non-fiction ☐

GENRE:		☆☆☆☆☆
SUBJECT:		☆☆☆☆☆
CHARACTERS:		☆☆☆☆☆
PLOT:		☆☆☆☆☆
READABILITY SCORE:		☆☆☆☆☆

Inspiration tree

Why I read it?

☆ MY REVIEW:

It inspired me to:

_____
_____
_____

Who will I recommend it to?

_____
_____
_____
_____
_____
_____

FAVORITE QUOTES FROM THIS BOOK:

hardcover   paperback   ebook   audiobook

OVERALL RATING: ☆☆☆☆☆

TITLE: _____ PUB DATE: _____

AUTHOR: _____ PAGE COUNT: _____

DATE STARTED: _____ DATE FINISHED: _____

SOURCE: _____ Bought ☐ Loaned ☐

Fiction ☐   Non-fiction ☐

GENRE:		☆☆☆☆☆
SUBJECT:		☆☆☆☆☆
CHARACTERS:		☆☆☆☆☆
PLOT:		☆☆☆☆☆
READABILITY SCORE:		☆☆☆☆☆

Inspiration tree

Why I read it?

☆ MY REVIEW:

It inspired me to:

Who will I
recommend it
to?

_____
_____
_____
_____
_____
_____
_____
_____
_____
_____
_____

FAVORITE QUOTES FROM THIS BOOK:

hardcover   paperback   ebook   audiobook

OVERALL RATING: ☆☆☆☆☆

TITLE: ─────────────────── PUB DATE: ─────────

AUTHOR: ────────────────── PAGE COUNT: ───────

DATE STARTED: ───────────── DATE FINISHED: ─────

SOURCE: ──────────────────

Bought ☐ Loaned ☐

Fiction ☐   Non-fiction ☐

GENRE:		☆☆☆☆☆
SUBJECT:		☆☆☆☆☆
CHARACTERS:		☆☆☆☆☆
PLOT:		☆☆☆☆☆
READABILITY SCORE:		☆☆☆☆☆

Inspiration tree

Why I read it?

☆ MY REVIEW:

It inspired me to:

Who will I
recommend it
to?

FAVORITE QUOTES FROM THIS BOOK:

hardcover   paperback   ebook   audiobook

OVERALL RATING: ☆☆☆☆☆

TITLE: _____ PUB DATE: _____

AUTHOR: _____ PAGE COUNT: _____

DATE STARTED: _____ DATE FINISHED: _____

SOURCE: _____ Bought ☐ Loaned ☐

Fiction ☐   Non-fiction ☐

GENRE:		☆☆☆☆☆
SUBJECT:		☆☆☆☆☆
CHARACTERS:		☆☆☆☆☆
PLOT:		☆☆☆☆☆
READABILITY SCORE:		☆☆☆☆☆

Inspiration tree

Why I read it?

It inspired me to:

Who will I recommend it to?

☆ MY REVIEW:

_____
_____
_____
_____
_____
_____
_____
_____
_____
_____
_____

FAVORITE QUOTES FROM THIS BOOK:

hardcover   paperback   ebook   audiobook

OVERALL RATING: ☆☆☆☆☆

TITLE: _____ PUB DATE: _____

AUTHOR: _____ PAGE COUNT: _____

DATE STARTED: _____ DATE FINISHED: _____

SOURCE: _____ Bought ☐ Loaned ☐

Fiction ☐   Non-fiction ☐

GENRE:		☆☆☆☆☆
SUBJECT:		☆☆☆☆☆
CHARACTERS:		☆☆☆☆☆
PLOT:		☆☆☆☆☆
READABILITY SCORE:		☆☆☆☆☆

Inspiration tree

Why I read it?

☆ MY REVIEW:

It inspired me to:

_____

_____

_____

_____

Who will I
recommend it
to?

_____

_____

_____

_____

_____

_____

FAVORITE QUOTES FROM THIS BOOK:

hardcover   paperback   ebook   audiobook

OVERALL RATING: ☆☆☆☆☆

TITLE: _____ PUB DATE: _____

AUTHOR: _____ PAGE COUNT: _____

DATE STARTED: _____ DATE FINISHED: _____

SOURCE: _____ Bought ☐ Loaned ☐

Fiction ☐   Non-fiction ☐

GENRE:		☆☆☆☆☆
SUBJECT:		☆☆☆☆☆
CHARACTERS:		☆☆☆☆☆
PLOT:		☆☆☆☆☆
READABILITY SCORE:		☆☆☆☆☆

Inspiration tree

Why I read it?

It inspired me to:

Who will I recommend it to?

☆ MY REVIEW:

_____
_____
_____
_____
_____
_____
_____
_____
_____
_____
_____

FAVORITE QUOTES FROM THIS BOOK:

hardcover   paperback   ebook   audiobook

OVERALL RATING: ☆☆☆☆☆

TITLE: _____ PUB DATE: _____

AUTHOR: _____ PAGE COUNT: _____

DATE STARTED: _____ DATE FINISHED: _____

SOURCE: _____ Bought ☐ Loaned ☐

Fiction ☐   Non-fiction ☐

GENRE:		☆☆☆☆☆
SUBJECT:		☆☆☆☆☆
CHARACTERS:		☆☆☆☆☆
PLOT:		☆☆☆☆☆
READABILITY SCORE:		☆☆☆☆☆

Inspiration tree

Why I read it?

☆ MY REVIEW:

It inspired me to:

_____

_____

_____

Who will I
recommend it
to?

_____

_____

_____

_____

_____

_____

FAVORITE QUOTES FROM THIS BOOK:

hardcover   paperback   ebook   audiobook

OVERALL RATING: ☆☆☆☆☆

TITLE: _____   PUB DATE: _____

AUTHOR: _____   PAGE COUNT: _____

DATE STARTED: _____   DATE FINISHED: _____

SOURCE: _____   Bought [ ]   Loaned [ ]

Fiction [ ]   Non-fiction [ ]

GENRE:		☆☆☆☆☆
SUBJECT:		☆☆☆☆☆
CHARACTERS:		☆☆☆☆☆
PLOT:		☆☆☆☆☆
READABILITY SCORE:		☆☆☆☆☆

Inspiration tree

☆ MY REVIEW:

Why I read it?

It inspired me to:

Who will I recommend it to?

_____
_____
_____
_____
_____
_____
_____
_____
_____
_____
_____

FAVORITE QUOTES FROM THIS BOOK:

hardcover   paperback   ebook   audiobook

OVERALL RATING: ☆☆☆☆☆

TITLE: _____ PUB DATE: _____

AUTHOR: _____ PAGE COUNT: _____

DATE STARTED: _____ DATE FINISHED: _____

SOURCE: _____ Bought ☐ Loaned ☐

Fiction ☐   Non-fiction ☐

GENRE:		☆☆☆☆☆
SUBJECT:		☆☆☆☆☆
CHARACTERS:		☆☆☆☆☆
PLOT:		☆☆☆☆☆
READABILITY SCORE:		☆☆☆☆☆

Inspiration tree

Why I read it?

☆ MY REVIEW:

It inspired me to:

_____

_____

_____

Who will I
recommend it
to?

_____

_____

_____

_____

_____

FAVORITE QUOTES FROM THIS BOOK:

hardcover   paperback   ebook   audiobook

OVERALL RATING: ☆☆☆☆☆

TITLE: —————————— PUB DATE: ——————

AUTHOR: ————————— PAGE COUNT: ————

DATE STARTED: ———————— DATE FINISHED: ————

SOURCE: ——————————— Bought ☐ Loaned ☐

Fiction ☐ Non-fiction ☐

GENRE:		☆☆☆☆☆
SUBJECT:		☆☆☆☆☆
CHARACTERS:		☆☆☆☆☆
PLOT:		☆☆☆☆☆
READABILITY SCORE:		☆☆☆☆☆

Inspiration tree

Why I read it?

It inspired me to:

Who will I recommend it to?

⭐ MY REVIEW:

_____
_____
_____
_____
_____
_____
_____
_____
_____
_____

FAVORITE QUOTES FROM THIS BOOK:

hardcover   paperback   ebook   audiobook

OVERALL RATING: ☆☆☆☆☆

TITLE: _____   PUB DATE: _____

AUTHOR: _____   PAGE COUNT: _____

DATE STARTED: _____   DATE FINISHED: _____

SOURCE: _____   Bought ☐   Loaned ☐

Fiction ☐   Non-fiction ☐

GENRE:		☆☆☆☆☆
SUBJECT:		☆☆☆☆☆
CHARACTERS:		☆☆☆☆☆
PLOT:		☆☆☆☆☆
READABILITY SCORE:		☆☆☆☆☆

Inspiration tree

Why I read it?

☆ MY REVIEW:

It inspired me to:

_____

_____

_____

_____

Who will I
recommend it
to?

_____

_____

_____

_____

_____

FAVORITE QUOTES FROM THIS BOOK:

hardcover   paperback   ebook   audiobook

OVERALL RATING: ☆☆☆☆☆

TITLE: _____ PUB DATE: _____

AUTHOR: _____ PAGE COUNT: _____

DATE STARTED: _____ DATE FINISHED: _____

SOURCE: _____ Bought ☐ Loaned ☐

Fiction ☐ Non-fiction ☐

GENRE:		☆☆☆☆☆
SUBJECT:		☆☆☆☆☆
CHARACTERS:		☆☆☆☆☆
PLOT:		☆☆☆☆☆
READABILITY SCORE:		☆☆☆☆☆

Inspiration tree

Why I read it?

☆ MY REVIEW:

It inspired me to:

Who will I recommend it to?

_____
_____
_____
_____
_____
_____
_____
_____
_____
_____

FAVORITE QUOTES FROM THIS BOOK:

hardcover   paperback   ebook   audiobook

OVERALL RATING: ☆☆☆☆☆

TITLE: _____ PUB DATE: _____

AUTHOR: _____ PAGE COUNT: _____

DATE STARTED: _____ DATE FINISHED: _____

SOURCE: _____ Bought ☐ Loaned ☐

Fiction ☐   Non-fiction ☐

GENRE:		☆☆☆☆☆
SUBJECT:		☆☆☆☆☆
CHARACTERS:		☆☆☆☆☆
PLOT:		☆☆☆☆☆
READABILITY SCORE:		☆☆☆☆☆

Inspiration tree

☆ MY REVIEW:

Why I read it?

_____

_____

It inspired me to:

_____

_____

_____

Who will I recommend it to?

_____

_____

_____

FAVORITE QUOTES FROM THIS BOOK:

hardcover   paperback   ebook   audiobook

OVERALL RATING: ☆☆☆☆☆

TITLE: _____ PUB DATE: _____

AUTHOR: _____ PAGE COUNT: _____

DATE STARTED: _____ DATE FINISHED: _____

SOURCE: _____ Bought ☐ Loaned ☐

Fiction ☐   Non-fiction ☐

GENRE:		☆☆☆☆☆
SUBJECT:		☆☆☆☆☆
CHARACTERS:		☆☆☆☆☆
PLOT:		☆☆☆☆☆
READABILITY SCORE:		☆☆☆☆☆

Inspiration tree

Why I read it?

☆ MY REVIEW:

It inspired me to:

_____
_____
_____
_____
_____

Who will I recommend it to?

_____
_____
_____
_____
_____

FAVORITE QUOTES FROM THIS BOOK:

hardcover   paperback   ebook   audiobook

OVERALL RATING: ☆☆☆☆☆

TITLE: _____   PUB DATE: _____

AUTHOR: _____   PAGE COUNT: _____

DATE STARTED: _____   DATE FINISHED: _____

SOURCE: _____   Bought ☐   Loaned ☐

Fiction ☐   Non-fiction ☐

GENRE:		☆☆☆☆☆
SUBJECT:		☆☆☆☆☆
CHARACTERS:		☆☆☆☆☆
PLOT:		☆☆☆☆☆
READABILITY SCORE:		☆☆☆☆☆

Inspiration tree

Why I read it?

☆ MY REVIEW:

It inspired me to:

_____

_____

_____

Who will I recommend it to?

_____

_____

_____

FAVORITE QUOTES FROM THIS BOOK:

hardcover   paperback   ebook   audiobook

OVERALL RATING: ☆☆☆☆☆

TITLE: _____ PUB DATE: _____

AUTHOR: _____ PAGE COUNT: _____

DATE STARTED: _____ DATE FINISHED: _____

SOURCE: _____ Bought ☐ Loaned ☐

Fiction ☐ Non-fiction ☐

GENRE:		☆☆☆☆☆
SUBJECT:		☆☆☆☆☆
CHARACTERS:		☆☆☆☆☆
PLOT:		☆☆☆☆☆
READABILITY SCORE:		☆☆☆☆☆

Inspiration tree

Why I read it?

☆ MY REVIEW:

It inspired me to:

_____

_____

_____

Who will I
recommend it
to?

_____

_____

_____

_____

_____

FAVORITE QUOTES FROM THIS BOOK:

hardcover   paperback   ebook   audiobook

OVERALL RATING: ☆☆☆☆☆

TITLE: _____ PUB DATE: _____

AUTHOR: _____ PAGE COUNT: _____

DATE STARTED: _____ DATE FINISHED: _____

SOURCE: _____ Bought ☐ Loaned ☐

Fiction ☐   Non-fiction ☐

GENRE:		☆☆☆☆☆
SUBJECT:		☆☆☆☆☆
CHARACTERS:		☆☆☆☆☆
PLOT:		☆☆☆☆☆
READABILITY SCORE:		☆☆☆☆☆

Inspiration tree

Why I read it?

☆ MY REVIEW:

It inspired me to:

_____
_____
_____

Who will I recommend it to?

_____
_____
_____
_____
_____
_____
_____

FAVORITE QUOTES FROM THIS BOOK:

hardcover   paperback   ebook   audiobook

OVERALL RATING: ☆☆☆☆☆

TITLE: ————————————— PUB DATE: —————————

AUTHOR: ———————————— PAGE COUNT: —————————

DATE STARTED: —————————— DATE FINISHED: —————————

SOURCE: ————————————

Bought ☐ Loaned ☐

Fiction ☐   Non-fiction ☐

GENRE:		☆☆☆☆☆
SUBJECT:		☆☆☆☆☆
CHARACTERS:		☆☆☆☆☆
PLOT:		☆☆☆☆☆
READABILITY SCORE:		☆☆☆☆☆

Inspiration tree

Why I read it?

☆ MY REVIEW:

It inspired me to:

Who will I
recommend it
to?

FAVORITE QUOTES FROM THIS BOOK:

hardcover   paperback   ebook   audiobook

OVERALL RATING: ☆☆☆☆☆

TITLE: ——————————— PUB DATE: ———————

AUTHOR: —————————— PAGE COUNT: ———————

DATE STARTED: ——————— DATE FINISHED: ———————

SOURCE: —————————— Bought ☐ Loaned ☐

Fiction ☐   Non-fiction ☐

GENRE:		☆☆☆☆☆
SUBJECT:		☆☆☆☆☆
CHARACTERS:		☆☆☆☆☆
PLOT:		☆☆☆☆☆
READABILITY SCORE:		☆☆☆☆☆

Inspiration tree

Why I read it?

☆ MY REVIEW:

It inspired me to:

_____

_____

_____

Who will I
recommend it
to?

_____

_____

_____

_____

_____

_____

FAVORITE QUOTES FROM THIS BOOK:

hardcover   paperback   ebook   audiobook

OVERALL RATING: ☆☆☆☆☆

TITLE: _____ PUB DATE: _____

AUTHOR: _____ PAGE COUNT: _____

DATE STARTED: _____ DATE FINISHED: _____

SOURCE: _____ Bought ☐   Loaned ☐

Fiction ☐   Non-fiction ☐

GENRE:		☆☆☆☆☆
SUBJECT:		☆☆☆☆☆
CHARACTERS:		☆☆☆☆☆
PLOT:		☆☆☆☆☆
READABILITY SCORE:		☆☆☆☆☆

Inspiration tree

Why I read it?

☆ MY REVIEW:

It inspired me to:

_____

_____

_____

Who will I
recommend it
to?

_____

_____

_____

_____

_____

FAVORITE QUOTES FROM THIS BOOK:

hardcover   paperback   ebook   audiobook

OVERALL RATING: ☆☆☆☆☆

TITLE: _____ PUB DATE: _____

AUTHOR: _____ PAGE COUNT: _____

DATE STARTED: _____ DATE FINISHED: _____

SOURCE: _____ Bought ☐ Loaned ☐

Fiction ☐   Non-fiction ☐

GENRE:		☆☆☆☆☆
SUBJECT:		☆☆☆☆☆
CHARACTERS:		☆☆☆☆☆
PLOT:		☆☆☆☆☆
READABILITY SCORE:		☆☆☆☆☆

Inspiration tree

Why I read it?

☆ MY REVIEW:

It inspired me to:

_____
_____
_____
_____

Who will I recommend it to?

_____
_____
_____
_____
_____

FAVORITE QUOTES FROM THIS BOOK:

hardcover   paperback   ebook   audiobook

OVERALL RATING: ☆☆☆☆☆

TITLE: _____ PUB DATE: _____

AUTHOR: _____ PAGE COUNT: _____

DATE STARTED: _____ DATE FINISHED: _____

SOURCE: _____ Bought ☐ Loaned ☐

Fiction ☐   Non-fiction ☐

GENRE:		☆☆☆☆☆
SUBJECT:		☆☆☆☆☆
CHARACTERS:		☆☆☆☆☆
PLOT:		☆☆☆☆☆
READABILITY SCORE:		☆☆☆☆☆

Inspiration tree

Why I read it?

☆ MY REVIEW:

It inspired me to:

Who will I
recommend it
to?

FAVORITE QUOTES FROM THIS BOOK:

hardcover   paperback   ebook   audiobook

OVERALL RATING: ☆☆☆☆☆

TITLE: _____ PUB DATE: _____

AUTHOR: _____ PAGE COUNT: _____

DATE STARTED: _____ DATE FINISHED: _____

SOURCE: _____ Bought ☐ Loaned ☐

Fiction ☐   Non-fiction ☐

GENRE:		☆☆☆☆☆
SUBJECT:		☆☆☆☆☆
CHARACTERS:		☆☆☆☆☆
PLOT:		☆☆☆☆☆
READABILITY SCORE:		☆☆☆☆☆

Inspiration tree

Why I read it?

☆ MY REVIEW:

It inspired me to:

_____

_____

_____

Who will I
recommend it
to?

_____

_____

_____

_____

_____

FAVORITE QUOTES FROM THIS BOOK:

hardcover   paperback   ebook   audiobook

OVERALL RATING: ☆☆☆☆☆

TITLE: _____   PUB DATE: _____

AUTHOR: _____   PAGE COUNT: _____

DATE STARTED: _____   DATE FINISHED: _____

SOURCE: _____   Bought ☐   Loaned ☐

Fiction ☐   Non-fiction ☐

GENRE:		☆☆☆☆☆
SUBJECT:		☆☆☆☆☆
CHARACTERS:		☆☆☆☆☆
PLOT:		☆☆☆☆☆
READABILITY SCORE:		☆☆☆☆☆

Inspiration tree

Why I read it?

☆ MY REVIEW:

It inspired me to:

_____

_____

_____

_____

Who will I
recommend it
to?

_____

_____

_____

_____

FAVORITE QUOTES FROM THIS BOOK:

hardcover   paperback   ebook   audiobook

OVERALL RATING: ☆☆☆☆☆

TITLE: _____ PUB DATE: _____

AUTHOR: _____ PAGE COUNT: _____

DATE STARTED: _____ DATE FINISHED: _____

SOURCE: _____ Bought ☐ Loaned ☐

Fiction ☐   Non-fiction ☐

GENRE:		☆☆☆☆☆
SUBJECT:		☆☆☆☆☆
CHARACTERS:		☆☆☆☆☆
PLOT:		☆☆☆☆☆
READABILITY SCORE:		☆☆☆☆☆

Inspiration tree

Why I read it?

☆ MY REVIEW:

It inspired me to:

_____

_____

_____

_____

Who will I
recommend it
to?

_____

_____

_____

_____

FAVORITE QUOTES FROM THIS BOOK:

hardcover   paperback   ebook   audiobook

OVERALL RATING: ☆☆☆☆☆

TITLE: _____ PUB DATE: _____

AUTHOR: _____ PAGE COUNT: _____

DATE STARTED: _____ DATE FINISHED: _____

SOURCE: _____ Bought ☐ Loaned ☐

Fiction ☐   Non-fiction ☐

GENRE:		☆☆☆☆☆
SUBJECT:		☆☆☆☆☆
CHARACTERS:		☆☆☆☆☆
PLOT:		☆☆☆☆☆
READABILITY SCORE:		☆☆☆☆☆

Inspiration tree

Why I read it?

⭐ MY REVIEW:

It inspired me to:

_____
_____
_____

Who will I recommend it to?

_____
_____
_____
_____
_____

FAVORITE QUOTES FROM THIS BOOK:

hardcover   paperback   ebook   audiobook

OVERALL RATING: ☆☆☆☆☆

TITLE: _____   PUB DATE: _____

AUTHOR: _____   PAGE COUNT: _____

DATE STARTED: _____   DATE FINISHED: _____

SOURCE: _____   Bought ☐   Loaned ☐

Fiction ☐   Non-fiction ☐

GENRE:		☆☆☆☆☆
SUBJECT:		☆☆☆☆☆
CHARACTERS:		☆☆☆☆☆
PLOT:		☆☆☆☆☆
READABILITY SCORE:		☆☆☆☆☆

Inspiration tree

Why I read it?

☆ MY REVIEW:

It inspired me to:

Who will I recommend it to?

_____
_____
_____
_____
_____
_____
_____
_____
_____
_____
_____

FAVORITE QUOTES FROM THIS BOOK:

hardcover   paperback   ebook   audiobook

OVERALL RATING: ☆☆☆☆☆

TITLE: ——————————————— PUB DATE: ————————

AUTHOR: —————————————— PAGE COUNT: —————

DATE STARTED: ———————————— DATE FINISHED: —————

SOURCE: ————————————————

Bought ☐   Loaned ☐

Fiction ☐   Non-fiction ☐

GENRE:		☆☆☆☆☆
SUBJECT:		☆☆☆☆☆
CHARACTERS:		☆☆☆☆☆
PLOT:		☆☆☆☆☆
READABILITY SCORE:		☆☆☆☆☆

Inspiration tree

Why I read it?

It inspired me to:

Who will I recommend it to?

☆ MY REVIEW:

FAVORITE QUOTES FROM THIS BOOK:

hardcover   paperback   ebook   audiobook

OVERALL RATING: ☆☆☆☆☆

TITLE: _____ PUB DATE: _____

AUTHOR: _____ PAGE COUNT: _____

DATE STARTED: _____ DATE FINISHED: _____

SOURCE: _____ Bought ☐   Loaned ☐

Fiction ☐   Non-fiction ☐

GENRE:		☆☆☆☆☆
SUBJECT:		☆☆☆☆☆
CHARACTERS:		☆☆☆☆☆
PLOT:		☆☆☆☆☆
READABILITY SCORE:		☆☆☆☆☆

Inspiration tree

☆ MY REVIEW:

Why I read it?

It inspired me to:

_____
_____
_____
_____
_____
_____

Who will I recommend it to?

_____
_____
_____

FAVORITE QUOTES FROM THIS BOOK:

hardcover   paperback   ebook   audiobook

OVERALL RATING: ☆☆☆☆☆

TITLE: _____   PUB DATE: _____

AUTHOR: _____   PAGE COUNT: _____

DATE STARTED: _____   DATE FINISHED: _____

SOURCE: _____   Bought ☐   Loaned ☐

Fiction ☐   Non-fiction ☐

GENRE:		☆☆☆☆☆
SUBJECT:		☆☆☆☆☆
CHARACTERS:		☆☆☆☆☆
PLOT:		☆☆☆☆☆
READABILITY SCORE:		☆☆☆☆☆

Inspiration tree

Why I read it?

It inspired me to:

Who will I recommend it to?

☆ MY REVIEW:

_____
_____
_____
_____
_____
_____
_____
_____
_____

FAVORITE QUOTES FROM THIS BOOK:

hardcover   paperback   ebook   audiobook

OVERALL RATING: ☆☆☆☆☆

TITLE: _____   PUB DATE: _____

AUTHOR: _____   PAGE COUNT: _____

DATE STARTED: _____   DATE FINISHED: ___

SOURCE: _____   Bought ☐   Loaned ☐

Fiction ☐   Non-fiction ☐

GENRE:		☆☆☆☆☆
SUBJECT:		☆☆☆☆☆
CHARACTERS:		☆☆☆☆☆
PLOT:		☆☆☆☆☆
READABILITY SCORE:		☆☆☆☆☆

Inspiration tree

Why I read it?

☆ MY REVIEW:

It inspired me to:

_____

_____

_____

_____

Who will I
recommend it
to?

_____

_____

_____

_____

_____

FAVORITE QUOTES FROM THIS BOOK:

hardcover   paperback   ebook   audiobook

OVERALL RATING: ☆☆☆☆☆

TITLE: ———————————————— PUB DATE: ————————

AUTHOR: ——————————————— PAGE COUNT: —————

DATE STARTED: ————————— DATE FINISHED: ————

SOURCE: —————————————— Bought ☐ Loaned ☐

Fiction ☐   Non-fiction ☐

GENRE:		☆☆☆☆☆
SUBJECT:		☆☆☆☆☆
CHARACTERS:		☆☆☆☆☆
PLOT:		☆☆☆☆☆
READABILITY SCORE:		☆☆☆☆☆

Inspiration tree

☆ MY REVIEW:

Why I read it?

It inspired me to:

Who will I
recommend it
to?

FAVORITE QUOTES FROM THIS BOOK:

hardcover   paperback   ebook   audiobook

OVERALL RATING: ☆☆☆☆☆

TITLE: _____ PUB DATE: _____

AUTHOR: _____ PAGE COUNT: _____

DATE STARTED: _____ DATE FINISHED: _____

SOURCE: _____ Bought ☐   Loaned ☐

Fiction ☐   Non-fiction ☐

GENRE:		☆☆☆☆☆
SUBJECT:		☆☆☆☆☆
CHARACTERS:		☆☆☆☆☆
PLOT:		☆☆☆☆☆
READABILITY SCORE:		☆☆☆☆☆

Inspiration tree

Why I read it?

☆ MY REVIEW:

It inspired me to:

Who will I recommend it to?

FAVORITE QUOTES FROM THIS BOOK:

hardcover   paperback   ebook   audiobook

OVERALL RATING: ☆☆☆☆☆

TITLE: _____   PUB DATE: _____

AUTHOR: _____   PAGE COUNT: _____

DATE STARTED: _____   DATE FINISHED: _____

SOURCE: _____   Bought ☐   Loaned ☐

Fiction ☐   Non-fiction ☐

GENRE:		☆☆☆☆☆
SUBJECT:		☆☆☆☆☆
CHARACTERS:		☆☆☆☆☆
PLOT:		☆☆☆☆☆
READABILITY SCORE:		☆☆☆☆☆

Inspiration tree

Why I read it?

☆ MY REVIEW:

It inspired me to:

Who will I
recommend it
to?

_____

_____

_____

_____

_____

_____

_____

_____

_____

_____

_____

FAVORITE QUOTES FROM THIS BOOK:

hardcover   paperback   ebook   audiobook

OVERALL RATING: ☆☆☆☆☆

TITLE: _____ PUB DATE: _____

AUTHOR: _____ PAGE COUNT: _____

DATE STARTED: _____ DATE FINISHED: _____

SOURCE: _____ Bought ☐ Loaned ☐

Fiction ☐   Non-fiction ☐

GENRE:		☆☆☆☆☆
SUBJECT:		☆☆☆☆☆
CHARACTERS:		☆☆☆☆☆
PLOT:		☆☆☆☆☆
READABILITY SCORE:		☆☆☆☆☆

Inspiration tree

Why I read it?

It inspired me to:

Who will I recommend it to?

☆ MY REVIEW:

_____
_____
_____
_____
_____
_____
_____
_____
_____
_____

FAVORITE QUOTES FROM THIS BOOK:

hardcover   paperback   ebook   audiobook

OVERALL RATING: ☆☆☆☆☆

TITLE: _____   PUB DATE: _____

AUTHOR: _____   PAGE COUNT: _____

DATE STARTED: _____   DATE FINISHED: _____

SOURCE: _____   Bought ☐   Loaned ☐

Fiction ☐   Non-fiction ☐

GENRE:		☆☆☆☆☆
SUBJECT:		☆☆☆☆☆
CHARACTERS:		☆☆☆☆☆
PLOT:		☆☆☆☆☆
READABILITY SCORE:		☆☆☆☆☆

Inspiration tree

Why I read it?

☆ MY REVIEW:

It inspired me to:

_____

_____

Who will I
recommend it
to?

_____

_____

_____

_____

_____

_____

FAVORITE QUOTES FROM THIS BOOK:

hardcover   paperback   ebook   audiobook

OVERALL RATING: ☆☆☆☆☆

TITLE: _____ PUB DATE: _____

AUTHOR: _____ PAGE COUNT: _____

DATE STARTED: _____ DATE FINISHED: _____

SOURCE: _____ Bought ☐ Loaned ☐

Fiction ☐   Non-fiction ☐

GENRE:		☆☆☆☆☆
SUBJECT:		☆☆☆☆☆
CHARACTERS:		☆☆☆☆☆
PLOT:		☆☆☆☆☆
READABILITY SCORE:		☆☆☆☆☆

Inspiration tree

Why I read it?

☆ MY REVIEW:

It inspired me to:

Who will I recommend it to?

_____
_____
_____
_____
_____
_____
_____
_____
_____
_____

FAVORITE QUOTES FROM THIS BOOK:

hardcover   paperback   ebook   audiobook

OVERALL RATING: ☆☆☆☆☆

TITLE: _____ PUB DATE: _____

AUTHOR: _____ PAGE COUNT: _____

DATE STARTED: _____ DATE FINISHED: _____

SOURCE: _____ Bought ☐ Loaned ☐

Fiction ☐   Non-fiction ☐

GENRE:		☆☆☆☆☆
SUBJECT:		☆☆☆☆☆
CHARACTERS:		☆☆☆☆☆
PLOT:		☆☆☆☆☆
READABILITY SCORE:		☆☆☆☆☆

Inspiration tree

Why I read it?

It inspired me to:

Who will I recommend it to?

☆ MY REVIEW:

_____
_____
_____
_____
_____
_____
_____
_____
_____
_____

FAVORITE QUOTES FROM THIS BOOK:

hardcover   paperback   ebook   audiobook

OVERALL RATING: ☆☆☆☆☆

TITLE: _____ PUB DATE: _____

AUTHOR: _____ PAGE COUNT: _____

DATE STARTED: _____ DATE FINISHED: _____

SOURCE: _____ Bought ☐ Loaned ☐

Fiction ☐   Non-fiction ☐

GENRE:		☆☆☆☆☆
SUBJECT:		☆☆☆☆☆
CHARACTERS:		☆☆☆☆☆
PLOT:		☆☆☆☆☆
READABILITY SCORE:		☆☆☆☆☆

Inspiration tree

Why I read it?

☆ MY REVIEW:

It inspired me to:

_____

_____

_____

_____

_____

Who will I
recommend it
to?

_____

_____

_____

_____

FAVORITE QUOTES FROM THIS BOOK:

hardcover   paperback   ebook   audiobook

OVERALL RATING: ☆☆☆☆☆

TITLE: _____ PUB DATE: _____

AUTHOR: _____ PAGE COUNT: _____

DATE STARTED: _____ DATE FINISHED: _____

SOURCE: _____ Bought ☐ Loaned ☐

Fiction ☐   Non-fiction ☐

GENRE:		☆☆☆☆☆
SUBJECT:		☆☆☆☆☆
CHARACTERS:		☆☆☆☆☆
PLOT:		☆☆☆☆☆
READABILITY SCORE:		☆☆☆☆☆

Inspiration tree

Why I read it?

☆ MY REVIEW:

_____

_____

It inspired me to:

_____

_____

_____

Who will I recommend it to?

_____

_____

_____

_____

FAVORITE QUOTES FROM THIS BOOK:

hardcover   paperback   ebook   audiobook

OVERALL RATING: ☆☆☆☆☆

TITLE: _____ PUB DATE: _____

AUTHOR: _____ PAGE COUNT: _____

DATE STARTED: _____ DATE FINISHED: _____

SOURCE: _____ Bought ☐ Loaned ☐

Fiction ☐   Non-fiction ☐

GENRE:		☆☆☆☆☆
SUBJECT:		☆☆☆☆☆
CHARACTERS:		☆☆☆☆☆
PLOT:		☆☆☆☆☆
READABILITY SCORE:		☆☆☆☆☆

Inspiration tree

Why I read it?

☆ MY REVIEW:

It inspired me to:

_____
_____
_____
_____

Who will I recommend it to?

_____
_____
_____
_____
_____

FAVORITE QUOTES FROM THIS BOOK:

hardcover   paperback   ebook   audiobook

OVERALL RATING: ☆☆☆☆☆

TITLE: _____   PUB DATE: _____

AUTHOR: _____   PAGE COUNT: _____

DATE STARTED: _____   DATE FINISHED: _____

SOURCE: _____   Bought ☐   Loaned ☐

Fiction ☐   Non-fiction ☐

GENRE:		☆☆☆☆☆
SUBJECT:		☆☆☆☆☆
CHARACTERS:		☆☆☆☆☆
PLOT:		☆☆☆☆☆
READABILITY SCORE:		☆☆☆☆☆

Inspiration tree

Why I read it?

⭐ MY REVIEW:

It inspired me to:

Who will I recommend it to?

_____
_____
_____
_____
_____
_____
_____
_____
_____
_____

FAVORITE QUOTES FROM THIS BOOK:

hardcover   paperback   ebook   audiobook

OVERALL RATING: ☆☆☆☆☆

TITLE: _____   PUB DATE: _____

AUTHOR: _____   PAGE COUNT: _____

DATE STARTED: _____   DATE FINISHED: _____

SOURCE: _____

Bought ☐   Loaned ☐

Fiction ☐   Non-fiction ☐

GENRE:		☆☆☆☆☆
SUBJECT:		☆☆☆☆☆
CHARACTERS:		☆☆☆☆☆
PLOT:		☆☆☆☆☆
READABILITY SCORE:		☆☆☆☆☆

Inspiration tree

Why I read it?

☆ MY REVIEW:

It inspired me to:

Who will I recommend it to?

_____

FAVORITE QUOTES FROM THIS BOOK:

hardcover   paperback   ebook   audiobook

OVERALL RATING: ☆☆☆☆☆

TITLE: _____ PUB DATE: _____

AUTHOR: _____ PAGE COUNT: _____

DATE STARTED: _____ DATE FINISHED: _____

SOURCE: _____ Bought ☐   Loaned ☐

Fiction ☐   Non-fiction ☐

GENRE:		☆☆☆☆☆
SUBJECT:		☆☆☆☆☆
CHARACTERS:		☆☆☆☆☆
PLOT:		☆☆☆☆☆
READABILITY SCORE:		☆☆☆☆☆

Inspiration tree

Why I read it?

☆ MY REVIEW:

It inspired me to:

Who will I recommend it to?

FAVORITE QUOTES FROM THIS BOOK:

hardcover   paperback   ebook   audiobook

OVERALL RATING: ☆☆☆☆☆

TITLE: ———————————————— PUB DATE: ——————————

AUTHOR: ——————————————— PAGE COUNT: —————————

DATE STARTED: ————————— DATE FINISHED: ——————————

SOURCE: ————————————————

Bought ☐   Loaned ☐

Fiction ☐   Non-fiction ☐

GENRE:		☆☆☆☆☆
SUBJECT:		☆☆☆☆☆
CHARACTERS:		☆☆☆☆☆
PLOT:		☆☆☆☆☆
READABILITY SCORE:		☆☆☆☆☆

Inspiration tree

Why I read it?

☆ MY REVIEW:

It inspired me to:

Who will I
recommend it
to?

FAVORITE QUOTES FROM THIS BOOK:

hardcover   paperback   ebook   audiobook

OVERALL RATING: ☆☆☆☆☆

TITLE: _____ PUB DATE: _____

AUTHOR: _____ PAGE COUNT: _____

DATE STARTED: _____ DATE FINISHED: _____

SOURCE: _____ Bought ☐ Loaned ☐

Fiction ☐ Non-fiction ☐

GENRE:		☆☆☆☆☆
SUBJECT:		☆☆☆☆☆
CHARACTERS:		☆☆☆☆☆
PLOT:		☆☆☆☆☆
READABILITY SCORE:		☆☆☆☆☆

Inspiration tree

Why I read it?

☆ MY REVIEW:

It inspired me to:

_____

_____

_____

_____

_____

Who will I
recommend it
to?

_____

_____

_____

_____

FAVORITE QUOTES FROM THIS BOOK:

hardcover   paperback   ebook   audiobook

OVERALL RATING: ☆☆☆☆☆

TITLE: ——————————— PUB DATE: ———————

AUTHOR: ————————————— PAGE COUNT: ————

DATE STARTED: ——————————— DATE FINISHED: ————

SOURCE: ————————————— Bought ☐ Loaned ☐

Fiction ☐ Non-fiction ☐

GENRE:		☆☆☆☆☆
SUBJECT:		☆☆☆☆☆
CHARACTERS:		☆☆☆☆☆
PLOT:		☆☆☆☆☆
READABILITY SCORE:		☆☆☆☆☆

Inspiration tree

Why I read it?

☆ MY REVIEW:

It inspired me to:

———————————————
———————————————
———————————————

Who will I
recommend it
to?

———————————————
———————————————
———————————————
———————————————
———————————————
———————————————
———————————————
———————————————
———————————————

FAVORITE QUOTES FROM THIS BOOK:

hardcover   paperback   ebook   audiobook

OVERALL RATING: ☆☆☆☆☆

TITLE: _____ PUB DATE: _____

AUTHOR: _____ PAGE COUNT: _____

DATE STARTED: _____ DATE FINISHED: _____

SOURCE: _____ Bought ☐ Loaned ☐

Fiction ☐   Non-fiction ☐

GENRE:		☆☆☆☆☆
SUBJECT:		☆☆☆☆☆
CHARACTERS:		☆☆☆☆☆
PLOT:		☆☆☆☆☆
READABILITY SCORE:		☆☆☆☆☆

Inspiration tree

Why I read it?

It inspired me to:

Who will I recommend it to?

☆ MY REVIEW:

_____
_____
_____
_____
_____
_____
_____
_____
_____
_____

FAVORITE QUOTES FROM THIS BOOK:

hardcover   paperback   ebook   audiobook

OVERALL RATING: ☆☆☆☆☆

TITLE: _____ PUB DATE: _____

AUTHOR: _____ PAGE COUNT: _____

DATE STARTED: _____ DATE FINISHED: _____

SOURCE: _____ Bought ☐ Loaned ☐

Fiction ☐   Non-fiction ☐

GENRE:		☆☆☆☆☆
SUBJECT:		☆☆☆☆☆
CHARACTERS:		☆☆☆☆☆
PLOT:		☆☆☆☆☆
READABILITY SCORE:		☆☆☆☆☆

Inspiration tree

Why I read it?

☆ MY REVIEW:

It inspired me to:

_____

_____

_____

Who will I
recommend it
to?

_____

_____

_____

_____

_____

FAVORITE QUOTES FROM THIS BOOK:

hardcover   paperback   ebook   audiobook

OVERALL RATING: ☆☆☆☆☆

TITLE: _____ PUB DATE: _____

AUTHOR: _____ PAGE COUNT: _____

DATE STARTED: _____ DATE FINISHED: _____

SOURCE: _____ Bought ☐ Loaned ☐

Fiction ☐   Non-fiction ☐

GENRE:		☆☆☆☆☆
SUBJECT:		☆☆☆☆☆
CHARACTERS:		☆☆☆☆☆
PLOT:		☆☆☆☆☆
READABILITY SCORE:		☆☆☆☆☆

Inspiration tree

Why I read it?

☆ MY REVIEW:

It inspired me to:

_____

_____

_____

Who will I recommend it to?

_____

_____

_____

_____

_____

_____

_____

FAVORITE QUOTES FROM THIS BOOK:

hardcover   paperback   ebook   audiobook

OVERALL RATING: ☆☆☆☆☆

TITLE: _____ PUB DATE: _____

AUTHOR: _____ PAGE COUNT: _____

DATE STARTED: _____ DATE FINISHED: _____

SOURCE: _____ Bought ☐ Loaned ☐

Fiction ☐   Non-fiction ☐

GENRE:		☆☆☆☆☆
SUBJECT:		☆☆☆☆☆
CHARACTERS:		☆☆☆☆☆
PLOT:		☆☆☆☆☆
READABILITY SCORE:		☆☆☆☆☆

Inspiration tree

Why I read it?

☆ MY REVIEW:

It inspired me to:

_____

_____

_____

_____

Who will I
recommend it
to?

_____

_____

_____

_____

_____

FAVORITE QUOTES FROM THIS BOOK:

hardcover   paperback   ebook   audiobook

OVERALL RATING: ☆☆☆☆☆

TITLE: _____ PUB DATE: _____

AUTHOR: _____ PAGE COUNT: _____

DATE STARTED: _____ DATE FINISHED: _____

SOURCE: _____ Bought ☐ Loaned ☐

Fiction ☐   Non-fiction ☐

GENRE:		☆☆☆☆☆
SUBJECT:		☆☆☆☆☆
CHARACTERS:		☆☆☆☆☆
PLOT:		☆☆☆☆☆
READABILITY SCORE:		☆☆☆☆☆

Inspiration tree

Why I read it?

☆ MY REVIEW:

_____
_____
_____

It inspired me to:

_____
_____
_____

Who will I
recommend it
to?

_____
_____
_____
_____

FAVORITE QUOTES FROM THIS BOOK:

hardcover   paperback   ebook   audiobook

OVERALL RATING: ☆☆☆☆☆

TITLE: _____ PUB DATE: _____

AUTHOR: _____ PAGE COUNT: _____

DATE STARTED: _____ DATE FINISHED: _____

SOURCE: _____ Bought ☐ Loaned ☐

Fiction ☐   Non-fiction ☐

GENRE:		☆☆☆☆☆
SUBJECT:		☆☆☆☆☆
CHARACTERS:		☆☆☆☆☆
PLOT:		☆☆☆☆☆
READABILITY SCORE:		☆☆☆☆☆

Inspiration tree

Why I read it?

☆ MY REVIEW:

_____

_____

_____

It inspired me to:

_____

_____

_____

Who will I recommend it to?

_____

_____

_____

_____

_____

FAVORITE QUOTES FROM THIS BOOK:

hardcover   paperback   ebook   audiobook

OVERALL RATING: ☆☆☆☆☆

TITLE: _____ PUB DATE: _____

AUTHOR: _____ PAGE COUNT: _____

DATE STARTED: _____ DATE FINISHED: _____

SOURCE: _____ Bought ☐ Loaned ☐

Fiction ☐   Non-fiction ☐

GENRE:		☆☆☆☆☆
SUBJECT:		☆☆☆☆☆
CHARACTERS:		☆☆☆☆☆
PLOT·		☆☆☆☆☆
READABILITY SCORE:		☆☆☆☆☆

Inspiration tree

Why I read it?

☆ MY REVIEW:

It inspired me to:

_____

_____

Who will I recommend it to?

_____

_____

_____

_____

_____

FAVORITE QUOTES FROM THIS BOOK:

hardcover   paperback   ebook   audiobook

OVERALL RATING: ☆☆☆☆☆

TITLE: _____   PUB DATE: _____

AUTHOR: _____   PAGE COUNT: _____

DATE STARTED: _____   DATE FINISHED: _____

SOURCE: _____   Bought ☐   Loaned ☐

Fiction ☐   Non-fiction ☐

GENRE:		☆☆☆☆☆
SUBJECT:		☆☆☆☆☆
CHARACTERS:		☆☆☆☆☆
PLOT:		☆☆☆☆☆
READABILITY SCORE:		☆☆☆☆☆

Inspiration tree

Why I read it?

☆ MY REVIEW:

It inspired me to:

_____

_____

_____

Who will I
recommend it
to?

_____

_____

_____

_____

_____

_____

FAVORITE QUOTES FROM THIS BOOK:

hardcover   paperback   ebook   audiobook

OVERALL RATING: ☆☆☆☆☆

TITLE: _____   PUB DATE: _____

AUTHOR: _____   PAGE COUNT: _____

DATE STARTED: _____   DATE FINISHED: _____

SOURCE: _____   Bought ☐   Loaned ☐

Fiction ☐   Non-fiction ☐

GENRE:		☆☆☆☆☆
SUBJECT:		☆☆☆☆☆
CHARACTERS:		☆☆☆☆☆
PLOT:		☆☆☆☆☆
READABILITY SCORE:		☆☆☆☆☆

Inspiration tree

Why I read it?

☆ MY REVIEW:

It inspired me to:

_____

_____

_____

Who will I recommend it to?

_____

_____

_____

_____

_____

_____

FAVORITE QUOTES FROM THIS BOOK:

hardcover   paperback   ebook   audiobook

OVERALL RATING: ☆☆☆☆☆

TITLE: _____ PUB DATE: _____

AUTHOR: _____ PAGE COUNT: _____

DATE STARTED: _____ DATE FINISHED: _____

SOURCE: _____ Bought ☐ Loaned ☐

Fiction ☐   Non-fiction ☐

GENRE:		☆☆☆☆☆
SUBJECT:		☆☆☆☆☆
CHARACTERS:		☆☆☆☆☆
PLOT:		☆☆☆☆☆
READABILITY SCORE:		☆☆☆☆☆

Inspiration tree

Why I read it?

☆ MY REVIEW:

It inspired me to:

Who will I
recommend it
to?

FAVORITE QUOTES FROM THIS BOOK:

hardcover   paperback   ebook   audiobook

OVERALL RATING: ☆☆☆☆☆

TITLE: _____ PUB DATE: _____

AUTHOR: _____ PAGE COUNT: _____

DATE STARTED: _____ DATE FINISHED: _____

SOURCE: _____ Bought ☐ Loaned ☐

Fiction ☐ Non-fiction ☐

GENRE:		☆☆☆☆☆
SUBJECT:		☆☆☆☆☆
CHARACTERS:		☆☆☆☆☆
PLOT:		☆☆☆☆☆
READABILITY SCORE:		☆☆☆☆☆

Inspiration tree

Why I read it?

☆ MY REVIEW:

It inspired me to:

_____
_____
_____

Who will I recommend it to?

_____
_____
_____
_____
_____
_____

FAVORITE QUOTES FROM THIS BOOK:

hardcover   paperback   ebook   audiobook

OVERALL RATING: ☆☆☆☆☆

TITLE: _____ PUB DATE: _____

AUTHOR: _____ PAGE COUNT: _____

DATE STARTED: _____ DATE FINISHED: _____

SOURCE: _____ Bought ☐ Loaned ☐

Fiction ☐   Non-fiction ☐

GENRE:		☆☆☆☆☆
SUBJECT:		☆☆☆☆☆
CHARACTERS:		☆☆☆☆☆
PLOT:		☆☆☆☆☆
READABILITY SCORE:		☆☆☆☆☆

Inspiration tree

Why I read it?

☆ MY REVIEW:

It inspired me to:

_____
_____
_____

Who will I
recommend it
to?

_____
_____
_____
_____
_____

FAVORITE QUOTES FROM THIS BOOK:

hardcover   paperback   ebook   audiobook

OVERALL RATING: ☆☆☆☆☆

TITLE: _____ PUB DATE: _____

AUTHOR: _____ PAGE COUNT: _____

DATE STARTED: _____ DATE FINISHED: _____

SOURCE: _____ Bought ☐ Loaned ☐

Fiction ☐   Non-fiction ☐

GENRE:		☆☆☆☆☆
SUBJECT:		☆☆☆☆☆
CHARACTERS:		☆☆☆☆☆
PLOT:		☆☆☆☆☆
READABILITY SCORE:		☆☆☆☆☆

Inspiration tree

Why I read it?

☆ MY REVIEW:

It inspired me to:

_____

_____

_____

Who will I
recommend it
to?

_____

_____

_____

_____

_____

FAVORITE QUOTES FROM THIS BOOK:

hardcover   paperback   ebook   audiobook

OVERALL RATING: ☆☆☆☆☆

TITLE: _____ PUB DATE: _____

AUTHOR: _____ PAGE COUNT: _____

DATE STARTED: _____ DATE FINISHED: _____

SOURCE: _____ Bought ☐ Loaned ☐

Fiction ☐   Non-fiction ☐

GENRE:		☆☆☆☆☆
SUBJECT:		☆☆☆☆☆
CHARACTERS:		☆☆☆☆☆
PLOT:		☆☆☆☆☆
READABILITY SCORE:		☆☆☆☆☆

Inspiration tree

Why I read it?

☆ MY REVIEW:

It inspired me to:

_____

_____

_____

Who will I recommend it to?

_____

_____

_____

FAVORITE QUOTES FROM THIS BOOK:

hardcover   paperback   ebook   audiobook

OVERALL RATING: ☆☆☆☆☆

TITLE: _____ PUB DATE: _____

AUTHOR: _____ PAGE COUNT: _____

DATE STARTED: _____ DATE FINISHED: _____

SOURCE: _____ Bought ☐ Loaned ☐

Fiction ☐   Non-fiction ☐

GENRE:		☆☆☆☆☆
SUBJECT:		☆☆☆☆☆
CHARACTERS:		☆☆☆☆☆
PLOT:		☆☆☆☆☆
READABILITY SCORE:		☆☆☆☆☆

Inspiration tree

Why I read it?

☆ MY REVIEW:

It inspired me to:

Who will I
recommend it
to?

_____
_____
_____
_____
_____
_____
_____
_____
_____
_____
_____

FAVORITE QUOTES FROM THIS BOOK:

hardcover   paperback   ebook   audiobook

OVERALL RATING: ☆☆☆☆☆

TITLE: _____ PUB DATE: _____

AUTHOR: _____ PAGE COUNT: _____

DATE STARTED: _____ DATE FINISHED: _____

SOURCE: _____ Bought ☐ Loaned ☐

Fiction ☐   Non-fiction ☐

GENRE:		☆☆☆☆☆
SUBJECT:		☆☆☆☆☆
CHARACTERS:		☆☆☆☆☆
PLOT:		☆☆☆☆☆
READABILITY SCORE:		☆☆☆☆☆

Inspiration tree

Why I read it?

☆ MY REVIEW:

It inspired me to:

_____
_____
_____
_____

Who will I
recommend it
to?

_____
_____
_____
_____
_____

FAVORITE QUOTES FROM THIS BOOK:

hardcover   paperback   ebook   audiobook

OVERALL RATING: ☆☆☆☆☆

TITLE: _____ PUB DATE: _____

AUTHOR: _____ PAGE COUNT: _____

DATE STARTED: _____ DATE FINISHED: _____

SOURCE: _____ Bought ☐ Loaned ☐

Fiction ☐ Non-fiction ☐

GENRE:		☆☆☆☆☆
SUBJECT:		☆☆☆☆☆
CHARACTERS:		☆☆☆☆☆
PLOT:		☆☆☆☆☆
READABILITY SCORE:		☆☆☆☆☆

Inspiration tree

Why I read it?

⭐ MY REVIEW:

It inspired me to:

_____
_____
_____
_____

Who will I recommend it to?

_____
_____
_____
_____
_____
_____

FAVORITE QUOTES FROM THIS BOOK:

hardcover   paperback   ebook   audiobook

OVERALL RATING: ☆☆☆☆☆

TITLE: _____ PUB DATE: _____

AUTHOR: _____ PAGE COUNT: _____

DATE STARTED: _____ DATE FINISHED: _____

SOURCE: _____ Bought ☐ Loaned ☐

Fiction ☐   Non-fiction ☐

GENRE:		☆☆☆☆☆
SUBJECT:		☆☆☆☆☆
CHARACTERS:		☆☆☆☆☆
PLOT:		☆☆☆☆☆
READABILITY SCORE:		☆☆☆☆☆

Inspiration tree

Why I read it?

☆ MY REVIEW:

It inspired me to:

_____
_____
_____

Who will I recommend it to?

_____
_____
_____
_____
_____

FAVORITE QUOTES FROM THIS BOOK:

hardcover   paperback   ebook   audiobook

OVERALL RATING: ☆☆☆☆☆

TITLE: ———————————— PUB DATE: ————————

AUTHOR: —————————————— PAGE COUNT: ——————

DATE STARTED: ———————— DATE FINISHED: ————————

SOURCE: ————————————

Bought ☐   Loaned ☐

Fiction ☐   Non-fiction ☐

GENRE:		☆☆☆☆☆
SUBJECT:		☆☆☆☆☆
CHARACTERS:		☆☆☆☆☆
PLOT:		☆☆☆☆☆
READABILITY SCORE:		☆☆☆☆☆

Inspiration tree

Why I read it?

☆ MY REVIEW:

It inspired me to:

Who will I
recommend it
to?

FAVORITE QUOTES FROM THIS BOOK:

hardcover   paperback   ebook   audiobook

OVERALL RATING: ☆☆☆☆☆

TITLE: _____ PUB DATE: _____

AUTHOR: _____ PAGE COUNT: _____

DATE STARTED: _____ DATE FINISHED: _____

SOURCE: _____ Bought ☐ Loaned ☐

Fiction ☐   Non-fiction ☐

GENRE:		☆☆☆☆☆
SUBJECT:		☆☆☆☆☆
CHARACTERS:		☆☆☆☆☆
PLOT:		☆☆☆☆☆
READABILITY SCORE:		☆☆☆☆☆

Inspiration tree

Why I read it?

☆ MY REVIEW:

It inspired me to:

Who will I recommend it to?

FAVORITE QUOTES FROM THIS BOOK:

hardcover   paperback   ebook   audiobook

OVERALL RATING: ☆☆☆☆☆

TITLE: _____   PUB DATE: _____

AUTHOR: _____   PAGE COUNT: _____

DATE STARTED: _____   DATE FINISHED: _____

SOURCE: _____   Bought ☐   Loaned ☐

Fiction ☐   Non-fiction ☐

GENRE:		☆☆☆☆☆
SUBJECT:		☆☆☆☆☆
CHARACTERS:		☆☆☆☆☆
PLOT:		☆☆☆☆☆
READABILITY SCORE:		☆☆☆☆☆

Inspiration tree

Why I read it?

☆ MY REVIEW:

It inspired me to:

Who will I
recommend it
to?

_____
_____
_____
_____
_____
_____
_____
_____
_____
_____
_____

FAVORITE QUOTES FROM THIS BOOK:

hardcover   paperback   ebook   audiobook

OVERALL RATING: ☆☆☆☆☆

TITLE: _____ PUB DATE: _____

AUTHOR: _____ PAGE COUNT: _____

DATE STARTED: _____ DATE FINISHED: _____

SOURCE: _____ Bought ☐ Loaned ☐

Fiction ☐   Non-fiction ☐

GENRE:		☆☆☆☆☆
SUBJECT:		☆☆☆☆☆
CHARACTERS:		☆☆☆☆☆
PLOT:		☆☆☆☆☆
READABILITY SCORE:		☆☆☆☆☆

Inspiration tree

Why I read it?

☆ MY REVIEW:

It inspired me to:

_____

_____

_____

_____

_____

Who will I recommend it to?

_____

_____

_____

_____

FAVORITE QUOTES FROM THIS BOOK:

hardcover   paperback   ebook   audiobook

OVERALL RATING: ☆☆☆☆☆

TITLE: _____ PUB DATE: _____

AUTHOR: _____ PAGE COUNT: _____

DATE STARTED: _____ DATE FINISHED: _____

SOURCE: _____ Bought ☐ Loaned ☐

Fiction ☐   Non-fiction ☐

GENRE:		☆☆☆☆☆
SUBJECT:		☆☆☆☆☆
CHARACTERS:		☆☆☆☆☆
PLOT:		☆☆☆☆☆☆
READABILITY SCORE:		☆☆☆☆☆

Inspiration tree

Why I read it?

☆ MY REVIEW:

It inspired me to:

_____
_____
_____

Who will I
recommend it
to?
_____
_____
_____
_____

FAVORITE QUOTES FROM THIS BOOK:

hardcover   paperback   ebook   audiobook

OVERALL RATING: ☆☆☆☆☆

TITLE: _____ PUB DATE: _____

AUTHOR: _____ PAGE COUNT: _____

DATE STARTED: _____ DATE FINISHED: _____

SOURCE: _____ Bought ☐ Loaned ☐

Fiction ☐   Non-fiction ☐

GENRE:		☆☆☆☆☆
SUBJECT:		☆☆☆☆☆
CHARACTERS:		☆☆☆☆☆
PLOT:		☆☆☆☆☆
READABILITY SCORE:		☆☆☆☆☆

Inspiration tree

Why I read it?

☆ MY REVIEW:

It inspired me to:

_____

_____

_____

Who will I
recommend it
to?

_____

_____

_____

_____

_____

FAVORITE QUOTES FROM THIS BOOK:

hardcover   paperback   ebook   audiobook

OVERALL RATING: ☆☆☆☆☆

TITLE: _____ PUB DATE: _____

AUTHOR: _____ PAGE COUNT: _____

DATE STARTED: _____ DATE FINISHED: _____

SOURCE: _____ Bought ☐ Loaned ☐

Fiction ☐   Non-fiction ☐

GENRE:		☆☆☆☆☆
SUBJECT:		☆☆☆☆☆
CHARACTERS:		☆☆☆☆☆
PLOT:		☆☆☆☆☆
READABILITY SCORE:		☆☆☆☆☆

Inspiration tree

Why I read it?

☆ MY REVIEW:

It inspired me to:

_____

_____

_____

Who will I
recommend it
to?

_____

_____

_____

_____

_____

FAVORITE QUOTES FROM THIS BOOK:

hardcover   paperback   ebook   audiobook

OVERALL RATING: ☆☆☆☆☆

TITLE: _____ PUB DATE: _____

AUTHOR: _____ PAGE COUNT: _____

DATE STARTED: _____ DATE FINISHED: _____

SOURCE: _____ Bought ☐ Loaned ☐

Fiction ☐   Non-fiction ☐

GENRE:		☆☆☆☆☆
SUBJECT:		☆☆☆☆☆
CHARACTERS:		☆☆☆☆☆
PLOT:		☆☆☆☆☆
READABILITY SCORE:		☆☆☆☆☆

Inspiration tree

Why I read it?

☆ MY REVIEW:

It inspired me to:

_____
_____
_____
_____

Who will I
recommend it
to?

_____
_____
_____
_____
_____

FAVORITE QUOTES FROM THIS BOOK:

hardcover   paperback   ebook   audiobook

OVERALL RATING: ☆☆☆☆☆

TITLE: _____ PUB DATE: _____

AUTHOR: _____ PAGE COUNT: _____

DATE STARTED: _____ DATE FINISHED: _____

SOURCE: _____ Bought ☐ Loaned ☐

Fiction ☐   Non-fiction ☐

GENRE:		☆☆☆☆☆
SUBJECT:		☆☆☆☆☆
CHARACTERS:		☆☆☆☆☆
PLOT:		☆☆☆☆☆
READABILITY SCORE:		☆☆☆☆☆

Inspiration tree

Why I read it?

It inspired me to:

Who will I recommend it to?

☆ MY REVIEW:

_____
_____
_____
_____
_____
_____
_____
_____
_____
_____
_____

FAVORITE QUOTES FROM THIS BOOK:

hardcover   paperback   ebook   audiobook

OVERALL RATING: ☆☆☆☆☆

TITLE: _____   PUB DATE: _____

AUTHOR: _____   PAGE COUNT: _____

DATE STARTED: _____   DATE FINISHED: _____

SOURCE: _____   Bought ☐   Loaned ☐

Fiction ☐   Non-fiction ☐

GENRE:		☆☆☆☆☆
SUBJECT:		☆☆☆☆☆
CHARACTERS:		☆☆☆☆☆
PLOT:		☆☆☆☆☆
READABILITY SCORE:		☆☆☆☆☆

Inspiration tree

Why I read it?

☆ MY REVIEW:

It inspired me to:

Who will I recommend it to?

FAVORITE QUOTES FROM THIS BOOK:

hardcover   paperback   ebook   audiobook

OVERALL RATING: ☆☆☆☆☆

TITLE: _____   PUB DATE: _____

AUTHOR: _____   PAGE COUNT: _____

DATE STARTED: _____   DATE FINISHED: _____

SOURCE: _____   Bought ☐   Loaned ☐

Fiction ☐   Non-fiction ☐

GENRE:		☆☆☆☆☆
SUBJECT:		☆☆☆☆☆
CHARACTERS:		☆☆☆☆☆
PLOT:		☆☆☆☆☆
READABILITY SCORE:		☆☆☆☆☆

Inspiration tree

Why I read it?

☆ MY REVIEW:

It inspired me to:

_____
_____
_____
_____
_____

Who will I recommend it to?

_____
_____
_____
_____
_____

FAVORITE QUOTES FROM THIS BOOK:

hardcover   paperback   ebook   audiobook

OVERALL RATING: ☆☆☆☆☆

TITLE: _____ PUB DATE: _____

AUTHOR: _____ PAGE COUNT: _____

DATE STARTED: _____ DATE FINISHED: _____

SOURCE: _____ Bought ☐ Loaned ☐

Fiction ☐   Non-fiction ☐

GENRE:		☆☆☆☆☆
SUBJECT:		☆☆☆☆☆
CHARACTERS:		☆☆☆☆☆
PLOT:		☆☆☆☆☆
READABILITY SCORE:		☆☆☆☆☆

Inspiration tree

Why I read it?

It inspired me to:

Who will I recommend it to?

☆ MY REVIEW:

_____
_____
_____
_____
_____
_____
_____
_____
_____
_____

FAVORITE QUOTES FROM THIS BOOK:

hardcover   paperback   ebook   audiobook

OVERALL RATING: ☆☆☆☆☆

TITLE: _____ PUB DATE: _____

AUTHOR: _____ PAGE COUNT: _____

DATE STARTED: _____ DATE FINISHED: _____

SOURCE: _____ Bought ☐ Loaned ☐

Fiction ☐   Non-fiction ☐

GENRE:		☆☆☆☆☆
SUBJECT:		☆☆☆☆☆
CHARACTERS:		☆☆☆☆☆
PLOT:		☆☆☆☆☆
READABILITY SCORE:		☆☆☆☆☆

Inspiration tree

Why I read it?

☆ MY REVIEW:

It inspired me to:

_____
_____
_____

Who will I
recommend it
to?

_____
_____
_____
_____
_____

FAVORITE QUOTES FROM THIS BOOK:

hardcover   paperback   ebook   audiobook

OVERALL RATING: ☆☆☆☆☆

TITLE: _____   PUB DATE: _____

AUTHOR: _____   PAGE COUNT: _____

DATE STARTED: _____   DATE FINISHED: _____

SOURCE: _____   Bought ☐   Loaned ☐

Fiction ☐   Non-fiction ☐

GENRE:		☆☆☆☆☆
SUBJECT:		☆☆☆☆☆
CHARACTERS:		☆☆☆☆☆
PLOT:		☆☆☆☆☆
READABILITY SCORE:		☆☆☆☆☆

Inspiration tree

Why I read it?

☆ MY REVIEW:

It inspired me to:

_____

_____

_____

_____

_____

Who will I recommend it to?

_____

_____

_____

_____

FAVORITE QUOTES FROM THIS BOOK:

hardcover   paperback   ebook   audiobook

OVERALL RATING: ☆☆☆☆☆

TITLE: _____ PUB DATE: _____

AUTHOR: _____ PAGE COUNT: _____

DATE STARTED: _____ DATE FINISHED: _____

SOURCE: _____ Bought ☐   Loaned ☐

Fiction ☐   Non-fiction ☐

GENRE:		☆☆☆☆☆
SUBJECT:		☆☆☆☆☆
CHARACTERS:		☆☆☆☆☆
PLOT:		☆☆☆☆☆
READABILITY SCORE:		☆☆☆☆☆

Inspiration tree

Why I read it?

☆ MY REVIEW:

It inspired me to:

_____
_____
_____

Who will I
recommend it
to?

_____
_____
_____
_____
_____
_____

FAVORITE QUOTES FROM THIS BOOK:

hardcover   paperback   ebook   audiobook

OVERALL RATING: ☆☆☆☆☆

TITLE: _____ PUB DATE: _____

AUTHOR: _____ PAGE COUNT: _____

DATE STARTED: _____ DATE FINISHED: _____

SOURCE: _____ Bought ☐ Loaned ☐

Fiction ☐ Non-fiction ☐

GENRE:		☆☆☆☆☆
SUBJECT:		☆☆☆☆☆
CHARACTERS:		☆☆☆☆☆
PLOT:		☆☆☆☆☆
READABILITY SCORE:		☆☆☆☆☆

Inspiration tree

Why I read it?

☆ MY REVIEW:

It inspired me to: _____

Who will I recommend it to?

FAVORITE QUOTES FROM THIS BOOK:

hardcover   paperback   ebook   audiobook

OVERALL RATING: ☆☆☆☆☆

We hope
you enjoyed our book !

Our goal, as a small family company is making your
experience a great one.
There's nothing better than reading the valuable
feedback from you,
so please let us know if you like our book at :
eightidd@gmail.com
or leave a review with your thoughts about it.

Thanks for your amazing support !

CPSIA information can be obtained
at www.ICGtesting.com
Printed in the USA
LVHW051248100221
678898LV00003B/393

9 781716 280825